Taking on

Faith

in the City

by

David Newman

Assistant Curate, St. Mary's, Bushbury

GROVE BOOKS LIMITED

Bramcote   Nottingham   NG9 3DS

CONTENTS

Copyright the respective authors 1986

FOREWORD

Planning booklets of multiple authorship is never easy! When we first discussed this one as a group, we felt that our response to the ACUPA Report would concentrate on the challenge to the church, and we encouraged a parallel response from the Grove Ethics Group on the challenge to the nation. Their response is now published as *Hope in the City.* This overlaps with our booklet more than we had originally hoped, which leaves the national dimension to the Report under-considered. Nevertheless we hope that these two booklets along with the one in the Worship series – *Worship in the City* – will together provide a varied reflection on the Report and stimulate the debate in the church which has already begun.

QUOTATIONS

Extracts from the Report, *Faith in the City,* are reprinted by permission of the publishers, Church House Publishing. Feferences to 'the Report' always refer to *Faith in the City* unless otherwise mentioned. Numbered references with a colon (e.g. '5:5') are to numbered paragraphs in the Report.

THE COVER PICTURE
is by Peter Ashton

First Impression May 1986

ISSN 0144-171X
ISBN 1 85174 024 0

1. WHAT SORT OF NATION?

by John Root

'To reflect on the challenge which God may be making to Church and Nation' was part of the Commission's terms of reference. This dual focus is reflected in the Report's format: an introductory Part One deals with 'The Challenge', followed by more substantial Parts Two and Three . . . 'To the Church' and '. . . To the Nation', respectively. However, there is a danger of too strong a division between the two.

The church exists within the nation and is strongly shaped by it. just as in turn it seeks to shape the nation. An exclusively church-orientated report would have been a partial and incomplete one, albeit a more comfortable one, since it is the national aspects that have drawn on it the wrath of MPs and the Press. Here it is ironic to recall words written by Bishop David Sheppard in 1974:

> 'The bite of the gospel generally comes not when we stop at expounding Christian belief or principles, but when we go on to show that a change is needed in attitudes and actions. Paul was given a hearing in Jerusalem as long as he recounted his spiritual experiences. It was when he said that God sent him to the Gentiles that they shouted him down. He was touching then on the raw nerve of racial prejudice and the threat to their privileged position.'[1]

ACUPA has generated attention and controversy in a way that, for example, Archbishop Coggan's 'Call to the Nation' failed to do, largely because it has been more ready to speak of *change* in attitudes and actions.

Church and Context

Recognition of the major importance of the national context for the church's ministry in urban areas has certainly been the experience of many urban clergy, not least evangelical Anglicans, over the past three decades. Evangelicals, majored first on *conversion,* when following the success of Billy Graham's 1954 Harringay crusade, they increasingly sought to preach the same gospel in inner urban areas. The discovery that response was not as immediate as in suburban or student settings raised questions of *culture:* was the gospel being packaged and presented in wrong cultural forms? Impetus was given to such an approach by the 1967 National Evangelical Anglican Congress at Keele, and the correspondence on 'Christians in Industrial Areas' that grew out of it. Questions of technique, however, began to be over-shadowed by questions of *content:* perhaps the 'gospel' had in fact been overly shaped by a comparatively successful suburban context, whereas eyes needed opening to biblical emphases on social justice and God's concern for the oppressed, which several theologians (often not overtly evangelical) were increasingly majoring on. The formation of the Evangelical Coalition for Urban Mission (ECUM) in 1980 and its journal *City Cries* have reflected this development.

ACUPA's report indicates the same type of awareness across the Anglican spectrum: that the weakness of the church's life and witness in urban areas cannot simply by solved by 'more of the same' (4:6); rather that

1 David Sheppard *Built as a City* (Hodder, 1974) p.265.

experience of Urban Priority Areas poses an acute challenge to reconsider the nature and practice of our faith, and how that faith bears on the way our nation is organized. Only in the light of this context, the Report presupposes, can the church respond as its Lord would have it, to the deprivation of UPAs.

How Divided a Nation?

It is worth pausing at this point to examine the truth of this claim, for it is a highly divisive one, not least among evangelical Anglicans. Are there areas of correlated acute social misery and evangelistic ineffectiveness in this country? If so, is this due simply to either the foolishness and misfortune of those who live there, or from consciously chosen policies of the nation's leaders?

As regards the first question, the Report makes clear to any with the ears to hear the depth of misery that exists. The first chapter on 'Urban Priority Areas' (especially paragraph 18 onwards) gives the details of urban economic decline, unemployment, bad housing, social disintegration, and – most starkly – rates of illness and death. This evidence is amplified in Part 3, where alongside the bare statistics come glimmers of the personal shock experienced by members of the commission (largely 'establishment' and non-clerical let it be noted) at what they experienced, e.g.: 'Commission members in their visits to the major cities have seen bad housing of every description, and have been shaken by the experience' (10:5).

It is important that the force of this point be held on to. The 'comprehension gap' between 'comfortable' and 'uncomfortable' Britain[1] is a reality of fundamental importance in British society. On the one hand the church also experiences that gap ('the majority of the well-housed live in the ouer suburbs, well away from and ignorant of the conditions of the inner areas. Many church members share their ignorance,' the section on housing goes on to say – 10:104). On the other hand, the church, seeking to serve a God of truth and justice, has the responsibility to insist that this situation be felt and responded to. So the Report urges: 'The church as a whole can produce a more sensitive climate of public opinion' (5:85).

In reply to those who accuse it of lacking adequate expertise to speak on national and political affairs[2], one clear and indisputable qualification of the Church of England is simply that number of its clergy whose homes as well as their work is in UPAs. This is a qualification that no other national body has in anything like the same degree, and requires that the testimony of the Church of England is at least seriously listened to. Indeed this has been a traditional Anglican role. In 1834 the rector of St. Ebbe's, Oxford, W. W. Champneys preached:

> 'Perhaps you think the case not quite so bad: that it might have been so in times past, but that things are quite changed now. They who only pass through the great streets of a city, know not what they know who are amongst its courts and alleys'.[3]

1 The phrases come from Kenneth Leech and Bishop David Sheppard respectively.
2 As, for example, Brian Mawhinney M.P. in *Third Way* (January 1985) p.25.
3 Champneys was to come to prominence as the vicar of St. Mary's, Whitechapel (1837-60), and by the time of the 1851 Religious Census was the most outstandingly effective urban clergyman in the country. His words here are strikingly similar to Engels' description of the way urban poverty in Manchester was conveniently obscured. Champneys was, of course, too early to be labelled a Marxist.

A century and a half later it is not difficult to imagine a UPA clergyman seeking to persuade a suburban congregation in similar words.

Experience constantly shapes our thoughts — because acute deprivation is not consistently encountered by most people in Britan today, it tends not to affect how we think of our society. So that when, as happened in 1981 and 1985, serious violence breaks out in deprived areas, refuge is too easily taken in superficial explanations based on 'trouble-makers' and 'political agitators'. Such ignorance is compounded by our having the most politically biased press of the post-war period, so that the experience of both life and ministry in UPAs is constantly misunderstood. 'A huge sense of relief and joy that the problems they have been struggling with, often with feelings of guilt and failure, have been recognized at last' was one UPA clergyman's response to the Report.[1] Both the truth of the Report's account of life in UPAs and the emotional pain behind it, must be the starting point for 'taking on' the church's response to the Report.[2]

Acknowledging such experience may not prescribe the solution. A searingly painful account of suffering and injustice can be wrongly used to stampede people into accepting remedies without questions. Nonetheless when those representing comfortable Britain agree that the situation in UPAs is bad, reject as impracticable the solutions offered, and fail to produce effective alternatives of their own, one concludes that they are dangerously insulated from the experience of urban misery.

Church and Nation

Finally it is worth raising some points arising from the 'overlap' of national and church issues.

1   There is a clear contrast between the strongly factual 'Nation' section of the Report. and the much more hypothetical 'Church' section. The Commissioners are to be commended for in turn commissioning a survey of clergy (though too often they choose to take no further what was discovered — for example, about evangelical effectiveness, 2:26), but on the whole the Report illustrates how dismally uninformed and apparently unconcerned the Church of England is about what is really happening to it. For its recommendations to the church to carry real authority there needs to be a much fuller and more critically tested information base. That could well undermine several of the guiding principles of current Anglican leadership.

2   Is the Report *too* concerned for national as opposed to church issues (a ratio of almost exactly 3:2 as regards pages)? And does some of the hostility that the church faces today stem from the perception that it is more ready to make bold demands of others than of itself? The recommendation to the church to set up a £10 million Urban Fund is its most costly domestic recommendation. Set against the demands it makes of the nation is that not too modest? And will even

[1] Eddie Neale, in the *Church of England Newspaper*, (20 December 1985).
[2] A recent, powerful account of such pain is Pip Wilson's 'Gutter Feelings'. Until recently he was youth leader at the Mayflower Centre, Canning Town.

that be reached ? Frank Field, MP, writing to *The Times* (13 December 1985) urged use of the church's £1.7 billion assets to underwrite inner-city investment, and the move of its bureaucracy from Westminster to the inner-city.

3 Does the Report give insufficient weight to the importance of personal, spiritual change in bringing about national, social change? Does it betray loss of nerve about both the demand and the offer of the gospel? To someone burdened with the problems of life in a UPA such questions seem to open the door to pious evasion of necessary, costly political change; but for others 'To the extent that the Church of England's reputation for holiness is wanting . . ., its prescriptions for changes in the ordering of society will lack the weight claimed for them.'[1]

There is no greater enemy of wholesome moral debate in our society than polarization into strongly personal, socially conservative responses; and impersonal, strongly political ones. By contrast Scripture constantly interweaves personal holiness and political responsibility (Malachi 3.5 is a particularly concise example). The Report is rightly strong on the collective injustice that creates the misery of UPAs; but it seriously neglects the effects of personal sins, such as dishonesty, laziness, and sexual immorality. For example, the future of the black community is threatened not only by white racism but by its large proportion of unmarried mothers. The Report is right to emphasize racism, and to urge strategies of racism awareness training and affirmative action to combat it. It is timid in remaining silent on the similarly devastating damage to the future of the balck community caused by the lack of stable father-mother relationships.

More widely the report echoes conventional progressive piety inspeaking of 'single parents' as suffering from disadvantage, as unavoidable as old age or physical handicap; but is unwilling to identify the personal responsibility that often causes single parenthood. Digby Anderson wrote in *The Times* (10 December 1985) both of the Report's 'overwhelming neglect of the greatest existing source of welfare, the normal family', and of its lack of comparative analysis. It would be impoverishing to dismiss this as merely 'dry right' polemic. How have the disadvantaged – historically, internationally, and within contemporary Britain – improved their circumstances? The track record of the Report's type of solution is not unalloyed success. Building up personal moral restraint, family cohesion, and a sense of obligation to the national community have traditionally played major roles, and the Report loses by down-grading them comparatively.[2]

If the Church of England is to speak more 'prophetically' to our society, it must learn to unite the voices of collective responsibility and personal transformation. Whilst the Report is to be commended for saying unpopular things about the former, it has been too bound by the ground rules of secular debate to also speak the New Testament's word of personal rebuke, repentance and re-birth.

1 Clifford Longley *The Times* (30 December 1985).
2 Examples would include, from this country, the effect of evangelical non-conformity, especially Sunday Schools, on nineteenth century working class advancement; the growth in prosperity of the Jewish community; and currently the Gujerati community.

2. WHAT SORT OF THEOLOGY?

by Roger Sainsbury and John Holden

Theology has taken a front seat in responses to the Report. In a House of Commons debate on inner sities an MP criticized the report as 'short on theology' and an article in *The Times* commented: 'the theological discussion contained in the report demonstrates a profound lack of faith in the fundamental tenets of Christianity'. The Report itself speaks of 'an inescapable theological debate' and therefore those of us who support the Report must welcome the fact that its theology is being so actively debated. A right theology is vital for our ministry in the inner city. We are encouraged that the General Synod Standing Committee Report says, 'In the coming phase there is need, first, for theological reflection'.

The Place of the Bible

John Goldingay, speaking at the 1986 Anglican Evangelical Assembly, pointed out that evangelicals pride themselves in accepting the authority of the whole Bible but in practice they ignore parts of it. The authors of *Faith in the City* do not stress the authority of Scripture but in practice apply Scripture to many of the situations they address themselves to. Reading the chapter on 'Theological Priorities' one might be drawn to the conclusion that the Report is weak on biblical authority but embedded throughout it are statements that endorse its authority. (cf. 2:17, 9:28 9.57, 14:5.1).

This wide use of biblical authority covering the whole of life is to be welcomed particularly set against the often narrow application of biblical authority to matters of personal salvation and morals, that we find in some evangelical literature and preaching.

The chapter on Theological Priorities starts from the teaching of Jesus on showing compassion to those in need (3:1) and Paul's instructions in Galatians to 'remember the poor' (3:2). It sees the Old Testament Laws as 'attempting to impose a number of controls upon society' (3:1) and the prophets declaring a concern for 'social justice and the protection of the weak' (3:14).

We judge that this chapter would have had a greater impact if specific biblical passages on these subjects had been expounded in relation to the challenge of UPAs today. Biblical authority needs to be laid alongside human experience.

In a footnote the Base Communities of Latin America are commended as having 'Their primary focus in shared Bible study' (p.80). The whole Report encourages biblical study and theological reflection (3:36) in a refreshing way that is linked to human experience. In Frontier Youth Trust this has led to what has been called 'Underside Theology' as the scriptures have been studied with powerless and deprived young people in our UPAs. At St. Matthew's Walsall, in the Justice Group, we looked at the Bible and reflected theologically on a whole range of justice issues. e.g. unemployment, poverty, racism, punishment, etc.[1] The Bible has come

[1] cf. Roger Sainsbury *Justice on the Agenda* (Marshalls).

alive for the first time with some members of the group, not in discussing matters of personal salvation but in pursuing matters of social justice. 'I never realized the Bible had so much to say on justice' exclaimed an excited social worker.

Personal and Social

The Report's case rests on the belief that there are significant areas of our country 'where we are confronted by an acute form of relative poverty — officially recognized as "multiple deprivation" ' (3:3). Here is need on a major scale which requires a direct response to the teaching of Jesus to show compassion to those in need. The Report affirms that 'The example of the Good Samaritan creates an imperative. It is impossible to be a Christian without responding, in some way or other, to the neighbour who is in need' (3:2). This personal dimension of the gospel is further affirmed in 'the infinite worth of one sinner who repents . . . to bring people a message of repentance, forgiveness and personal transformation that is addressed to the heart and mind of each one of us' (3:6). This initial commitment to evangelism is not elaborated on in the rest of the Report. The understandable, and in our view correct, emphasis, is on the need for Christian social justice. The gospel we proclaim must be relevant to the context of the Urban Priority Areas. However, this does leave the Report open to the criticism that the major question of evangelism is left begging! For, while we seek social justice and cross the road to bring relief to those in Urban Priority Areas, we still face the question 'How are people to live their lives of integrity and faith, hope and joy, under the heavy hand of injustice, prejudice and deprivation?' One is reminded here of William Temple's saying, 'If we have to choose between making men Christian, and the social order more Christian, we have to choose the former, but there is no such antithesis'. In the light of this saying, the Report leaves us with the strong impression that if we give ourselves wholeheartedly to the latter, we achieve the former! Our experience shows that this is not the case. We are commissioned by our Saviour Christ to make disciples. The challenge in the Urban Priority Areas, as elsewhere, is fundamentally evangelistic. As we teach others to obey Christ's commands, we discover what it means to follow Christ in the Urban Priority Areas, and we go on to discover the real felt needs of our neighbour, spiritual and social, private and corporate.

The demand for obedience in the Great Commission in Matthew 28, leads us to commitment to three strands of scripture which belong together — working for social justice, evangelism, and serving needs. In 3:42 evangelism is not given a distinctive place, and in the chapter as a whole, there is not a clarification between this and serving other needs. It is inadequate to put them under the heading 'personal' as if they were the same thing.

Love Incarnate

The Report affirms 'such is the incarnational or "embodied" character of our religion, that we cannot seriously envisage a Christian concern which leaves out of account the physical and social conditions under which people actually live'. We want to uphold this emphasis. We desire 'to be the protagonist of (Christian) social change' and involved in 'challenging those in power and risking the loss of our own power' (3:7). The Report contrasts the church's preference for 'ambulance work' with an unwillingness 'to rectify injustices in the structures of society' (3:7). While it may be true that some do not mind 'being cast in the role of protector and helper of the weak and powerless' it cannot be shown that 'No-one minds' (3:7). Neither can it be shown that everyone's motive is to retain a 'superior position and one's power of free decision'. When fighting a war, an army has to care for its casualties and even accept a responsibility for those of the enemy! The tension of priorities in war is just as acute for those committed to working for social change, serving needs, and seeking to win new disciples in the Urban Priority Areas. This is particularly true for those living there long term. The tension is painful, and sometimes a cross.

There is another tension. We would reject two exclusive approaches. The first which says (in effect) you must first convert the world before you can change it. and the second which says (in effect) you must first change the structures of society before you can convert anyone. It is not uncommon to find as many of those who subscribe to the latter as do to the former. Too many from within the church who have sympathy with either of these two approaches, betray insufficient experience of actually living alongside people in Urban Priority Areas, for a sufficient length of time to work through the tensions. The fundamental biblical truth is that an incarnational theology affirms a belief in love, and the power of love.

A significant lesson can be learnt from another Christian Urban statement in this country, albeit nearly a hundred years ago – *In Darkest England and The Way Out* by General Booth and the Salvation Army. This was a veritable *tour de force*. A direct result was to raise money for urban aid and change the laws relating to many things through challenging the Nation's conscience. Initially it incurred the wrath of those consciences. However, that 'Report', with all the work and commitment that lay behind it, was a living parable of incarnate love, and the power of that Christian love, when it is relevant, compassionate and totally addressed to the personal and social needs of the poor.

Members of the Commission were greatly moved by the scale of commitment which they found in the Urban Priority Areas. Within the church, the cost to clergy and their families is huge. It is known, though not mentioned in the Report, that one UPA parish invited over forty applicants to be incumbent before the offer was taken up! It is always costly on the frontiers of mission. The gospel has a lot to say about means as well as ends. So it will be certain characteristics of love incarnate which make for a breakthrough for the gospel and the kingdom. They particularly include: perceived motives; the way we go about things; whether we really persevere; and whether we have a spirituality which by God's grace has the touch of the Master.

Judgment on Nations and Systems

The Report states: 'there is ample precedent in Christian tradition for exposing the system we have to moral judgment' (3:16). This tradition is found both in the Old and New Testaments. Old Testament prophets such as Amos and Isaiah majored on judgment of nations and economic systems.

They saw God as active in society and the need for the people of God to recognize that activity particularly in terms of judgment. Jesus' presence in the world was a judgment on nations and systems, both secular and religious. His crucifixion was a focus of the judgment (John 3.16-19). God continues his work of judgment now by his Holy Spirit – 'And when the Spirit comes, he will convince the world concerning sin and righteousness and judgment' (John 16.8).

Demonic systems in society come under judgment when God's Spirit is active. We saw this during the Evangelical Revival with the demonic systems of slavery and child labour. In a General Synod report Charles Elliott comments: 'a Spirit-filled Church that rejoices in tongues and warm fellowship of the Spirit, but neglects the hard task of prophesying against the powers of darkness as they manifest themselves in our society opens itself to the question of whether it is being faithful to the Spirit in which it exults'.

Michael Cassidy describes an experience of being anointed with the Spirit, leading to a realization that 'our national sin is discrimination on the basis of race' and 'unless we repent of this sin and of this system, the judgments of history will become the judgment of God upon us'.[1]

What is true of South Africa and apartheid can equally be true of injustice in our UPAs. Graham Dow argues that 'Satan seeks to destroy man in the West by ruling over him through economic power structures'.[2] If the Holy Spirit is active, these structures will come under judgment as the Report suggests they should.

Place of Repentance

In a *Sunday Telegraph* article – 'Hell, Sin and Inner Cities' – Peregrine Worsthorne pointed out that there is no mention of sin and repentance in the Report or that 'inner-city dwellers may be suffering deprivation because of God's wrath at their wrong-doing'. We share his concern about the failure to mention sin, but reckon the call to repentance in the Bible goes with responsibility and is primarily an activity of the powerful not the powerless. Any call to repentance must be seen therefore against the background of what the Report calls the 'prevailing sense of powerlessness' in UPAs (p.xiv).

The call to repentance in both the Old Testament prophets and in the ministry of John the Baptist, is directed towards the secular and religious powers of the day, and not primarily to the broken and the oppressed. Our experience in UPAs is that the majority of people are 'sinned against' as well as being sinners. Therefore, first and foremost, we must reveal a gospel of 'acceptance' and 'unjudgmental friendship' – 'This man welcomes sinners and eats with them' (Luke 16.2).

It is perhaps worth remembering that Peter points out 'judgment begins with the house of God' (1 Peter 4.17). It is sad that the press has presented the Report as primarily calling for U-turns from the Government, when its primary application should be a call for the church to repent of its

---

1 Michael Cassidy *Bursting The Wineskins* (Hodder, 1983) p.121.
2 G. Dow *Dark Satanic Mills* (Shaftesbury Project, 1979) p.22.

failure to UPAs. Biblical repentance does not just involve sorrow for failure, but actions in terms of compassion, justice in financial matters and right use of resources (Luke 3.10-14). As the church shows that its repentance is genuine, it can call on the nation to repent.

The Power of the Gospel

The Report states – 'The church has the full authority of the Gospel . . . to bring people a message of repentance, forgiveness and personal transformation' (3:6). But in its discussion of the gospel in UPAs the Report rightly points out there should be a different emphasis – 'it would stress the drama of the passion and crucifixion rather than any intellectual formulation of the Doctrine of Atonement' (3:36). We think that there is a whole area of theological work that needs following through here, which the Report leaves undone. In Pip Wilson's book *Gutter Feelings* (13.123) he quotes a list of differences that need exploring with regard to our understanding of the gospel:

Middle Class	Working Class
Formulas	Drama
Theory	Action (Practices)
Status (Right with God)	Active Goodness
Personal Righteousness	Social Justice
Omnipotent God	Human Jesus

This is not a different gospel, but the same gospel seen from different vantage points. This might provide agenda for the Doctrine Commission. There also seems to be a theological weakness in the Report in its failure to recognize the importance of the Holy Spirit. John Wimber has recently pointed out 'Any system or force that must be overcome, in order for the gospel to be believed, is cause for a power encounter'. In evangelism in UPAs the 'poor in spirit' will see their need of the Holy Spirit's power, if the gospel is to be believed. We must, however, get away from the triumphalist approach and identify with the powerlessness of UPA people:
'It is when we acknowledge ourselves as powerless . . . it is then that we become penetrable by the Spirit of God. As long as we imagine that the world can be changed by our activities, our good works, our energy, we substitute our effort for the power of God' (Charles Elliott).

Faithful Sowing or Successful Reaping

We have already noted the theological statement 'The measure of Church success is an elusive concept . . . a more biblical criterion of faithfulness is required' (2:17). Set alongside this we must place the statement that 'mission involves a clear commitment to promoting Church growth' (4:18). There is a tension here for evangelicals, that was reflected in the 1986 General Synod debate. Bishop David Sheppard commented – 'There has been no golden age of church going in UPAs and let us not trick ourselves that there is some magic formula'. But Roger Godin moved an amendment – 'unashamedly affirming that the Christian Gospel, when faithfully proclaimed in word and deed, effects a transformation of individual lives, of families and communities'. It is important we abandon the 'theology of quick success' and 'easy answers'. Many traditional

11

Western methods of evangelism cut little ice in these areas, and as we have already indicated, we need to ask questions both about the nature of the Christian gospel, and also what we mean by faithful proclamation. Because these questions are being faced, local indigenous Christian communities are growing and witnessing to the gospel and the kingdom in UPAs. Ultimately the question is not 'success', but significance for the kingdom.

A Balanced Theology

What sort of theology? The Report specifically criticizes our theology which has 'always' been deductive and academic. We welcome this criticism and the Report's recommendation of a wide-ranging review of theological training. It is when a strong academic emphasis is allied to an exclusively deductive approach that an unbalanced theology results. Few could support a theology which merely holds up a set of propositions, or a catechism to be learnt. However, the Report does not give a biblical basis for its disagreement with deduction, and even less for its apparent support for a thoroughgoing (if not exclusively) inductive approach. We believe this wrong because the biblical picture is both deductive because of revelation, and inductive because of experience. It is not a case of half and half, but rather a special blending of the two. Neither is it a case of starting deductively and then changing to an inductive theology. There is an interplay between the two because we move between what scripture teaches us, and what the Holy Spirit teaches those who are obedient in the situation. Our theology is deductive because of revelation, in creation 'In the beginning God created . . .' In Christ – 'You are the Christ, the Son of the living God . . . flesh and blood has not revealed this to you, but my Father who is in heaven' (Matthew 16.16-17). Our theology is deductive because of Christ's teaching. The parable of the Good Samaritan; washing the disciples' feet; Jesus' teaching on salt and light; all these and many more are clear examples of deductive theology. The Great Commission and the two Great Commandments are classic examples of deductive theology.

It is as we take the first step of obedience that the inductive character of theology comes in. The Bible teaches us to go to people and start where they are. The situation will press us to decide on priorities making for a division of labour so that we do not 'give up preaching the word of God' or neglect widows in their need (Acts 6). But there are more direct references to this inductive nature of theology in the Bible. Our theology is inductive because Jesus teaches (John 8) we will only 'know the truth' and be set free by the truth when we hear and receive his order for . . . 'if you obey my teaching, you really are my disciples'. Only as we live among the poor, only as we hunger and thirst after righteousness among the poor, only as we dare to discover what it means to wash the feet of the poor, only as we obediently pray for healing, only as we faithfully share the saving truth of Jesus, only as we weep with the poor, only as we are touched and understand every facet of their impoverishment, will we ourselves know the revelance of the Gospel. This is its true inductive character. A wrong swing towards an exclusively inductive theology will undermine the revelation of God in Christ, and ultimately obscure that eternal life which is 'to know you the only true God, and Jesus Christ whom you have sent' (John 17.3).

3. WHAT SORT OF CHURCH?

by David Horn and David Newman

As we write, there are perhaps a million people in Lent house-groups across the nation, seeking to answer 'What on earth is the Church for?' The very title (the title of the B.C.C. publication which undergirds the course) is indicative of the questioning mood of today. Statistics of church life have undermined any confidence or presumption, and the ACUPA Report concludes that 'for the vast majority of people in the UPAs the Church of England – perhaps Christianity – is seen as irrelevant' (2:4). 'In places the survival of the church itself may be threatened' (4:1).

It is not just that whole groups within our society are not reached by the church – that can still sound as if these groups are there just to be reached or helped or whatever. It is that the church fails to see how unlike its true nature it has become if such groups are missing! A whole area of God's varied grace will not be on display. We can illustrate this from the church's relationship with the black community.

It has been argued that the renewed coming of black people after the war was the 'barium meal' that showed up the sicknesses of our society.[1] It has equally exposed a range of issues for the church (cf. 5:54-56).[2] It is very difficult to find a West Indian Christian who on entering Anglican Churches in those early days did not face antipathy and rejection. Many came with certificates of confirmation and letters of introduction to the mother church. Some were asked by the clergy not to come again, many found cardigans and coats on seats ensuring black people could not sit with white people. We can and must understand how fearful the congregations were. We can imagine the threat felt to their standards, their friendship groups, and their sense of tribal unity. But we cannot condone it. To condone it is to convert a gift of God into a problem.

Much primitive religion has a focus in some sort of 'totem' perhaps set in the centre of the community. It is something that symbolizes the art and the warfaring power of the tribe. It is somewhere to go in times of death, marriage, danger and birth. Conversely all that cuts across the tribal magic and custom is 'taboo' and is harshly repudiated. Wherever Christianity becomes improperly enmeshed with kinds of tribal customs it becomes a faith in which people celebrate their sameness rather than worship of the living God.[3]

Many black Christians have found it preferable to commute back to majority black churches rather than face a frozen welcome in their local churches. This only highlights a wider problem of cultural prejudice,

[1] cf. Peter Fryer *Staying Power: The History of Black People in Britain* (London, 1984).
[2] David Sheppard *Bias To The Poor* (Hodder, 1983) pp.60ff. J. and R. Wilkinson *Inheritors Together* (CIO, 1985) pp.12ff.
[3] Church growth writers have been crticized for encouraging the principle of the 'homogeneous unit' as most conducive to church growth – as in Donald McGavran *Understanding Church Growth* (Eerdmans, 1970) Chapter 11. His analysis of how groups have converted is, however most important, and he highlights the tension between fruitful discipling of groups and their integration one with the other.

however, and many working-class people find themselves similarly tolerated, patronized, and rejected by a middle-class church (4:5). The Report documents graphically how in both UPA and other parishes, black *and* working-class Christians are under-represented in congregation and leadership (figues 2.1 and 2.2 on pages 35-36) and we must add that this is not typical of the universal church at this time or through history.

This is the problem, or perhaps some would say the collusion in wickedness, that faces the church. It is certainly a denial of a church that knows not 'Jew or Greek, male or female, slave or free'. In the face of this, the Report offers a vision of a church that is 'local, outward-looking and participating' with a 'clear, ecumenical bias' (4:6), and it is to this vision we must now turn.

A local church . . .

A local church is seen in terms of 'having a firm commitment to the local people and to the places where they live, work and associate' (4:7). Three areas where this is worked out are in relation to location, culture, and leadership and ministry.

a) **Location** – The Report asks for a sensitivity to 'the neighbourhood' and suggests that there may be several different neighbourhoods within one parish, or neighbourhoods that actually cross parish boundaries (5:43ff.). Although the Anglican parochial system originally developed with such an awareness, it has been too inflexible as neighbourhoods have changed. New housing, a new road through a community, or different social centres, can all change the location of a neighbourhood and so, apart from boundary changes, the Report sees the possibility of 'small neighbourhood-based worship centres' and 'the development of centres, preferably ecumenical, in each neighbourhood (for example in house groups) which reach out in care and concern for the whole life of the neighbourhood and all its people' (5:45). Such a vision clearly presupposes an openness to lay leadership and ministry, and involves a radical decentralization of church life. Ways of developing this vision have been well written about elsewhere.[1]

b) **Culture** – The 'culture' of a church's life can be rather vague and difficult to define, but it is certainly true that ways of teaching, styles of worship, forms of meetings, etc. often tend to reflect a middle-class culture even in UPAs. In the area of worship, for instance, the Report gives some helpful ideas about how to make worship relevant to the *local* culture (6:101ff.) – attention to 'feelings' as well as thinking, involvement of the congregation, testimonies and stories, informality, a sensitivity to the harsh realities of urban life, etc. – and the drawbacks of using the large 1300-page Alternative Service Book are rightly noted.

Similarly ways of teaching need to be experience-based rather than academic and bookish, learning rather than teaching centred.[2] It is

1 cf. David Prior *The Church in the Home* (Marshalls, 1983) and *Sharing Pastoral Care in the Parish* (Grove Pastoral Series No. 3, 1980).
2 cf. David Gillett *How do Congregations Learn?* (Grove Booklet on Ministry and Worship No. 67, 1978).

a pity that the contribution of Pentecostalism and of the Charis-
matic movement has been largely ignored in the Report, for it would
seem to have a definite relevance here in three ways:

Firstly – the movement has rediscovered the nearness of God – as
Donald McGavran writes – 'the baptism of the Holy Spirit confers
upon very humble people the unshakeable conviction that he
is standing at their elbow to deliver them from dangers, comfort
them in sorrow and enable them to praise, witness and live as
children of God'.[1]

Secondly – the emphasis on the gifts of the Spirit leads to more local
involvement in ministry and contribution in worship rather than
the emphasis on educated natural giftedness that is so often
the case.

Thirdly – the Healing Ministry is becoming an important part of the
church's mission in some urban areas, providing signs of God's
grace and love to people who, as David Sheppard notes, 'are
much more likely to believe that God is infinitely distant from
them and all their doings.'[2]

c) **Leadership and ministry.** The ACUPA Report is committed to
shared ministry between clergy and laity. This is not new, for one of
the theological imperatives of the Tiller Report was that 'the lcoal
Church, as the Body of Christ in a particular place, should be responsible for undertaking the ministry of the gospel in its own areas'.[3]
It is now worked out with an urban slant, particularly through
  i)   a church leadership development programme.
  ii) local non-stipendiary ministry (LNSM).
  iii) training of the clergy.
For i) and iii) the key is appropriate training: courses that are geared
for urban life and ministry need to be developed so as to include the
widest range of ministry, including women and members of ethnic
groups.[4]

Clergy training will also need to develop an appropriate attitude to
ministry and leadership that seeks to draw out all that is good in the
local church and community. The role of Theological Colleges comes
under close scrutiny, where residential, academically orientated
training is questioned.

The development of LNSMs is a key recommendation. The Report
clearly sees this as an important step of encouragement for local
ministry, but it is equally possible that it could serve to perpetuate
the clergy/lay divide and so work against local ministry. There would
need to be some definition of which local ministries required ordin-
ation and which did not. The Report has a wide role for LNSMs –
'One might be appointed as the Priest responsible for an estate within
the Parish, including involvement in Community Groups, house

[1] *op. cit.* p.267.
[2] *op. cit.* p.202.
[3] John Tiller *A Strategy for the Church's Ministry* (CIO, 1983) p.48.
[4] cf. Clarry Hendrickse *One Inner Urban Church and Lay Ministry* (Grove Pastoral Series
No. 13, 1983).

groups and pastoral care. Another might be responsible for youth work' (6:39). It does not make clear though, why *lay* people could not do these jobs, or why LNSMs have to be limited to local ministry.

Alternatively could there not be a diaconate which would undertake basic local leadership in community work and service – even an ecumenical diaconate?[1] Our fear would be that LNSMs would perpetuate an unhelpful clericalism, although it does allow for local presidency of the eucharist which would be acceptable to the whole church in a way that lay presidency would not. The motive for the idea of LNSM would seem to be entirely positive, but needs more thinking through in practice. Anyway the presupposition of the whole argument is the presence of active local people in the churches, which is something that is often not the case. Consequently the second part of the vision assumes a vital importance.

An outward-looking church

An outward-looking vision requires 'an attentiveness to the individual and social realities of local life' (4:14) and a deep involvement in them. It also involves 'the clear commitment to promoting church growth' (4:18).

There would not seem to be any necessary dichotomy between these two aspects of mission, although the Report finds a tension 'between the view of the church as a group of committed Christians and our vision of an outward-looking as a group of committed Christians and our vision of an if necessary at the level of their folk religion' (4:16). If, as this seems to suggest, an outward-looking church is to let folk religion set the agenda for its ministry and mission, then its social involvement could well work against promoting church growth. Thus it is important to clarify the parameters of this involvement in relation to folk religion and the community.

a)   **Evangelism and discipleship.** The Report suggests that 'the outward-looking church must also include giving time willingly to baptisms and weddings and funerals' (4:16), yet to lump all these offices together suggests a lack of strategy – for they are very different in character. Baptism is a response to the Gospel – 'Do you turn to Christ?' – whereas weddings and funerals relate more to man in creation. From a creational perspective we certainly need to be involved in the social life of the community, affirming the value of people, as created by God, but we distort the gospel to say that it is no different. Could this be part of our failure to make committed Christians in UPAs? In one of our local churches (Church of the Good Shepherd, Low Hill – Parish of Bushbury) – 60% of the church council, including one warden, the secretary, and a Deanery Synod representative, have been converted in relation to a baptism policy related to visible discipleship. This church has real community involvement including a Youth Training Scheme, flats for homeless young people, and a welfare and rights unit, so that it is known to care, but *not* to baptize on demand. Often more time is given to people than if baptism was administered quickly and the impression given by the clergy is that

1 A suggestion by Richard G. Jones in *Methodist Recorder* (30 January 1986).

'this obviously means something to them'. It is strange that in the church we often have a strict policy in relation to communion but an open policy for baptism, whereas it is a common experience of groups that where the entrance is easy so is the exit. If such a baptism policy is handled creatively with the use of Thanksgiving services and suitable preparation, then the feelings of rejection that the Report seems to fear can be lessened. Indeed, confidence in the 'naked Gospel'[1] is an essential accompaniment of an outward-looking church – there can be forms of openness that deny the power of the gospel.

b) **Community involvement.** 'Community' is a concept that features frequently in the Report. It is a vital part of its local, outward-looking vision (4:7–4:12), a goal for intermediate action that could be defined as social concern with a human face (3:19), and a style of work that involves people (12:36). It is a 'warmly, persuasive word' that none-theless 'needs to be used with care'. While warmly endorsing the need for the church to be involved in the community, there are cautions that need to be expressed.

Firstly, community is not in itself a good thing. The strongest com-munities in the United Kingdom are probably those found in Northern Ireland, and where community links are strong, community fears can easily lead to polarization of people, with violence being condoned in the name of 'community'. This leads to the awareness that Christian community work must be checked by its involvement and vulnerability to the most vulnerable, otherwise it can so easily become selfish. There are examples, for instance, of white churches that finance the maintenance of their church halls by the needs of black people.

Secondly, it is important that doing things 'for' people does not become doing things 'to' them, and placing the recipients of help in patterns of bondage as bad as those they first knew. In the parable of the Samaritan on the Jericho to Jerusalem road, the outcast is the helper. Without the governing influence of the Holy Spirit, we tend to develop community action committees in which the Samaritans of our world are captive clients forced into gratitude for our help. For those who are disapproved of to be partners will require more than tea, sympathy and an enhanced Urban Aid Programme. It will require the eyes to *see* all God's co-workers and the courage to *challenge* them . . . Some of the harshest words of judgment in the Gospels are reserved for the person with one talent who yet failed to use it in the service of the master.

Thirdly, the isolation of clergy can trap them into accepting the wrong sort of help. With the absence of most diocesan officers and advisers from UPAs and lay support perhaps thin, the availability of govern-ment and other funds can seem very attractive, but they should not

---

1 This is the phrase used by John Finney when talking about Luke 10.4. He suggested that the Lord's instructions to the disciples about their mission were to make them rely on the 'naked gospel' alone.

be accepted and utilized without alert negotiations of the terms and conditions. The church can easily become cheap labour in the government-sponsored community care programme that can rob handicapped members of society of proper care, and trained professionals of paid employment (3:20, 8:62ff., 8:93, 12:24). Furthermore, we note that in recent months many government programmes have become very short-term or subject to significant changes in the terms and conditions.

Some of the most interesting examples of community development available are found in the books written by Dr. John Perkins.[1] He has lived the message before he has written it, and the results in terms of conversions, church training programmes and economic development are impressive. In Mendenhall, Mississippi, a church-based, black-led, multi-racial team, developed retail stores and health programmes that now offer a significant service to the whole community. In a 70% white community 50% of retail trade passes through their co-operative store.

There is a strong argument for Christians to ensure that alternative funding and alternative management structures are imaginatively considered before commitments are accepted, especially where buildings are involved. Some Christian projects could have been developed in secular forums. Some projects with secular funding should have been funded by the richer suburban churches. It is not hard to find small UPA congregations meeting in large community complexes. Many of them will tell you 'we've been had – we never wanted this'. They cannot understand the balance sheets and feel forced to elect the more administratively confident members of the congregations to office on the PCC and meanwhile they clean up the floors after the Social Services Departments luncheon club. Systems can be negotiated with the Charity Commissioners that have the members in control, and grants can be obtained that leave enough funding for the administration and the cleaning. We know of clergy that have been grateful to local authorities when congregations know they are being exploited.

One of the styles of community concern that has been used quite widely is that of St. Matthew's, Brixton, where the old church building has been refurbished inside and made available for a wide range of community functions. Clearly much has been achieved through this and David Sheppard commends it as a work of 'kenosis' or self-emptying. But there is an alternative conclusion – 'Is it in the interests of poor black worshippers to take control of the building out of their hands and to put it into the hands of others, many of whom are not committed to the church? Because the building equals power, the practice of turning church buildings in the black community into community centres is one way black people are disenfranchized. This diminishes rather than increases the power of black people in the Church of England'.[2]

[1] John Perkins A Quiet Revolution and With Justice for all (Regal Books).
[2] The opinion of Rev. David Moore, a former curate of St. Matthews, quoted in Inheritors Together (CIO, 1985) p.67.

c) **Audit for the Local Church.** This is one of the key recommendations of the Report (5:37 and appendix A) suggesting that UPA congregations need to learn before they act and that such an ordered learning process will help dioceses to plan, and will assist the Urban Fund with its allocation of resources. Initial indications are that diocesan committees like the sound of this. Two mistakes could be made:

a) In community and church development work in working class communities *'learning' must never be separated from action.* In one sense it never can be because when we study people we always do something to them. It is dangerous to suggest to a local church that it cannot act until it understands in an ordered way. If we would build up local Christians in their following of Christ in their communities we must first emphasize how much they already know and harness that in action and further *discovery.* The 'ACTION – DISCOVERY – PRAYER – REFLECTION – ACTION . . .' cycle must then continue for ever. This is not a six-months-to-one-year project.

b) The second fundamental error is to allow separation of local and wider issues. This is true of both reflection and action. It is not possible to understand what is happening in the locality without understanding what is happening in the city (e.g. Balsall Heath in Birmingham is often said to have a prostitution problem. In fact it is Birmingham which has the prostitution trade that is located in Balsall Heath with the majority of consumers and providers coming into the area). This 'dialogue' between the local, the city, the national and the international is crucial for any church wanting to become involved in any of the basic issues such as crime, education, housing, work and Social Security.[1]

Conclusion

We have sought to reflect on the Report's vision of a 'local, outward-looking, participating church', and while we thoroughly endorse the vision we note and question the underlying 'feel' that seems to pervade the Report, that if the church relates rightly to the community, then it will automatically prosper and be strong. In an effort to stress the church's involvement in Society, the Report seems reluctant to equally allow for its distinctiveness from Society. For the church to be true to itself and to fulfil its mission both are crucial. There can be no wholesome proclamation of the gospel of grace when the need to work for justice in society is neglected. This Report indicates a need for repentance leading to a new working out of the gospel of grace, for only the word of grace can empower for a task such as this.

[1] The material in the Report should be supplemented by some of the following:
  a) *From Awareness to Action* (Grove Books, 15p).
  b) 'City Seen' from Community Education Centre SCN (1975) 13 Northbrook Road SE13 (has useful bibliography – see also the Report p.368).
  c) 'Situation Analysis' UTU Worksheet No. 3. Urban Theology Unit, 210 Abbeyfield Road, Sheffield S47 AZ.
  d) Material from the Evangelical Urban Training Project, P.O. Box 83, Liverpool L69 8AN.
  In general, American material is conceptually more precise but *has* to be adapted. It is tempting to use British material unadapted, and this is usually a mistake.

4. WHAT SORT OF SHARING?

by Micahel Paget-Wilkes and Peter Hobson

1. Sharing between parishes

In discovering what life is like in UPAs the Report highlights the massive differences existing between UPA and suburban/rural churches. The serious gap that divides these different experiences of church life is clearly brought home to us. As well as living in a divided Britain we also are part of a divided church. Commenting on this, the Report rightly asserts that 'the quality of relationship between the UPA and the wider church is a supreme test of the life of the whole Body' (5:76). And 'unless the whole church can be persuaded to take seriously the challenge and plight of the church in the UPAs it will cease to be a church of the whole people' (5:77). The quality of relationship between the different parts of the church is seen as a kind of 'spiritual thermometer' for the overall life of the whole body.

Reasons for these divisions include fear between different cultures, geographical separation, the size and deep rooted nature of the division, the inability to see easy ways of solving the problem, and the reluctance of those with power and wealth to share it voluntarily. However, the publication of the Report appears significantly to have inspired considerable goodwill on both sides to seek ways of healing the divide. So, what practical steps can be taken that draw us closer into one body? The first step must be *educative* which, in turn, will lead to *sharing* and *growth.*

(i) The Report insists there is an important *learning* process that needs to take place. The wider church needs to begin to feel, experience and understand what it is like to live in a UPA (5:78). It is not sufficient to watch it on T.V. or pass through it on a commuter train. It is essential to gain firsthand experiences of the reality and harshness that comes from disintegrating housing, health, educational and environmental facilities, coupled with growing unemployment and deep-seated despair. It is essential to grasp that personal failure is not necessarily a result of personal laziness, selfishness or inability, but can also be caused by national, political and economic structures that predominately influence UPAs. It is also important not to think fatalistically that life in these areas will never change or that 'the problem' is too big to be solved. We need to affirm that Christian hope can lead to release from poverty.

(ii) One sad reflection is that the Report produced a weak section on how the wider church could learn to *share* and exchange with the UPA church (5:89). Of course there are difficulties involved but surely deeper and more understanding relationships between such churches must be the key factor in the uniting of a divided church. Exchange and sharing will firstly reduce the *fears* and barriers that exist at present. It will lead to people acknowledging each other as brothers and sisters in Christ, regardless of cultural differences. Theories, images and concepts of 'how the other half lives' can be transformed when we meet face to face. Fear of patronizing or being patronized, or buying off or being bought off through gifts of money, will be reduced through personal contact. The breaking down of such human barriers will show both the church itself, and the world, how the Body of Christ can indeed become a classless community. Only by coming together will we discover for ourselves the equality of all in the eyes of God.

Secondly, exchange and sharing needs to be seen as a *two-way process.* nsufficient is the idea that the strong church of the suburbs should distribute its 'goodies' to those in need. Every Christian community has both strengths and weaknesses.[1] Any *indepth* study of UPA and suburban churches will show there are major strengths in UPA churches, just as much as *vice versa.* What appears on the surface is often exactly the opposite underneath. The identification and sharing of gifts is needed on equal terms. Professional expertise and wealth exhibited in one large church can easily be shared in exchange for the level of commitment, the down-to-earth reality of faith, the determination to rejoice even under extreme pressure, the high level of Christian giving, the bluntness, honesty, corporate support found in a small pressurized UPA church. One example of this is 'incomers' reversing the trendy 'flight to the suburbs'. Encouraging 'incomers' to become involved in UPAs as learners as well as givers, careful not to stifle local leadership, acting possibly as link people with suburban churches elsewhere, can bring real benefits. Such commitment gives concrete embodiment to the biblical view that there is, in Christ, no between Jew and Greek, slave and freeman, white or balck, manager or worker and raises questions about totally homogeneous churches, be they black, working class or middle class.

Thirdly, by exchanging and sharing our different experiences of *suffering and pain* and the strength that Christ gives us to cope with these experiences, we will discover a new understanding of God's love that unites us together regardless of the human differences which separate us. Suffering is experienced in every Christian community in different forms, such as being mugged, living with children on the top of a tower block, experiencing hatred which flares into riot, death in the family, mental or physical handicap, terminal illness, depression, loneliness and pressure a work. Some forms are common to one area, others more prevalent in another. Suffering is experienced to certain depths or degrees, regardless of the particular form it may take. We need to learn to share with each other these different experiences of suffering, taking confidence by identifying each of our stiuations with Christ's suffering on the cross. This means that a wealthy educated judge's wife with a severely mentally handicapped child can begin to identify with a one-parent mother with four children under six in a tower block, or a West Indian mother with four youngsters and a husband unemployed. Christ's suffering on the cross for everyone can draw us all into inseparable love and support for each other regardless of the human and physical differences that we have. By sharing and exchanging such experiences we can discover a new unity in Christ through the very suffering that can strike us all at any time.

On the cross Christ intertwined his offer of new life with a preparedness to suffer for, and identify with, the weakest in the world. This Good News today, therefore, should balance 'a new life that encounters suffering with a suffering life that highlights salvation', or as John Perkins puts it, 'Our legitimacy and our identity as the church of Jesus Christ is wrapped up in our response to the victim in our world.' Or as Paul Tournier puts it, 'It is in suffering that I perceive Christ's nearness, his presence and his

1 cf. *Hope in the City* (Grove Ethics Series No. 61) Ch. 3.

participation in life.' So, just as the painful cross led Jesus to the joyful resurrection, becoming involved in the hurt of UPAs could show the wider church a new understanding of Christ's peace, power and glory today.

(iii) Just as learning across the social divide can lead to sharing, so too, deeper sharing between UPA churches and the wider church can lead to *growth.* Christian growth and maturity comes from Christ enabling us to do things that humanly speaking we could not do. Now, at present, there is a great divide between UPA and non-UPA parishes and people. Our natural inclination is to back off from any close involvement. However, as we face those seemingly insurmountable barriers, asking Christ to show us how we can draw closer to each other in understanding and unity, we will, in fact, *grow spiritually* as we discover what Christ unfolds before us. When Jesus talked to his disciples about following him he did not say to them *'accept* difficult situations if they come your way,' he said, 'make a conscious effort to *chose* the right and costly way,' i.e. 'If any man wants to come with me . . . he must take up his cross daily' (Luke 9.23).

If, therefore, we chose to face this painful division in our national church we will grow into new truth in Christ which we did not even know existed. We will be amazed at how much Christians with completely different social and cultural backgrounds actually have in common, how much we can enjoy each other's company and how much we can learn from each other, how much we will want to give to each other and how much richer life can be compared with sitting down in our own little cosy like-minded group. So sharing is not just an optional extra for those who have the time or inclination to do it. It is a basic, essential ingredient if we are to grow both as individual Christians and as the church of our nation.

2. Buildings
Understanding UPA parish life involves recognizing the immense impact of church buildings on each local church and community. The Report does not flinch when it states 'The question of church buildings in UPAs is serious, complex and intractable' (7:2). It goes on to describe the wide variety of difficulties brought on by old, cold, unsuitable buildings but sadly offers little real comfort or hope in its recommendations. The maintenance of large Victorican churches in terms of heating, lighting, repair and insurance are seen to be beyond the capacity of many UPA congregations (7:10). giving benefit to the community around, yet remaining the financial responsibility of the church alone (7:12).

The Report's solutions, (7:14-25) include:
(a) Sharing church buildings with other Christians (though the clash of 'peak worship times' often makes this difficult), with other faiths (which could be difficult for Christian converts from those faiths to accept), and with the local community (but with care to avoid the dangers as well as reaping the benefit from such associations).
(b) Developing an Urban Church Fund to finance adaptations and sharing arrangements. The Report does not go further to encourage a more radical rethink to discover a suitable theology for UPA church buildings. Surely, from the situation described, both parochial and diocesan levels need pointers toward practical ways forward ?

What would such a rethink involve? How does our view of traditional church buildings relate to biblical standards? What do we want our buildings to say? How can architecture express the nature of the church, the purpose of worship and the mission of the people of God? How would we implement, through our church buildings, our conviction that mission should indeed have priority over maintenance?

(1) Parish level

For example, take the following principles and their application affirmed recently by a UPA parish in Manchester:

Principles:
- (a)   The church is a pilgrim people not a fixed building.
- (b)   Churches are the home of a congregation not the house of God.
- (c)   Worshippers are participants not spectators.
- (d)   Ministry means service not status.
- (e)   The church's primary task is mission, not maintenance.
- (f)   Architecture is powerful, not neutral.
- (g)   Simplicity is not the enemy of beauty.
- (h)   Communion is a meal not a sacrifice.

Some points of application:

Therefore a church centre will:
* not promote any idea of 'holy places' in the building (a, b, h).
* not commit our successors to any one set concept of buildings for church life (a, b, e, f).
* encourage a flexible arrangement of furnishings (a, c).
* encourage seating arrangements where the congregation is 'gathered round' rather than in 'serried ranks' (a, c, h).
* provide for all the various activities of the congregation in addition to set worship (b, e).
* have acoustics which make it possible for vocal contribution from all present (c).
* not separate ministers from people other than is necessary for functional purposes (d).
* focus on the ministry offered rather than on the minister presiding (d, h).
* be available for use by the community throughout the week (e).
* have an entrance area which is welcoming (e, f), be responsible in the stewardship of the financial resources available to us (e, g).
* be aware of the potential impact on users of every aspect of its architecture and furnishings (f).
* seek to harness to the full the creative talents of our architect (initially) and of church members (thereafter) (g).

Consider the *positive and encouraging debate* as a parish sought to relate these ideas to their own building. Some points would be hard to implement, some costly, and others would take time to achieve, but the exercise would focus the congregation's thinking on the task facing the body of Christ and whether their church buildings actually enhanced or constrained the fulfilment of that task. They would then be in a far better position to know how to adapt, share or rebuild their plant so as to encourage and forward their primary task — to live and share God's Good News amongst the community.

TAKING ON FAITH IN THE CITY

Although the above principles refer mainly to the church's view of itself, the church would also need similarly to review its buildings in the light of local community needs. What facilities could be offered to the community which would both satisfy existing needs, draw church and community closer together and yet at the same time not diminish or weaken the presence, witness and growth of the Body of Christ? Such considerations of church buildings, both in relation to the church's own task and with the local community, would fully prepare it for any medium-or long-term decisions it may have to take.

(2) Diocesan level

Running parallel with creative parish thinking would be *diocesan resources* to service UPA parishes in this situation (7:58). Much closer liaison is needed between parish leadership and diocesan planners. This should not be limited just to the possible sale of church buildings (7:47). Such open consultation should be pressed further at every level of discussion regarding church buildings. Somehow the future needs to be shaped not just by Diocesan Committees but by genuine sharing, understanding, trust and agreement between committee and congregation. The Report's proposal of a UPA Redevelopment Officer (7:58) would encourage such a relationship, particularly if he were to 'assist the incumbent and the parish without wrestling all control from the local church' (7:58). Creative parish thinking and active diocesan support would then need to be *financed* to implement the decisions arrived at, e.g. through a Church Urban Fund (7:26).

(3) Finance

Reading Reports, finding out new facts and discovering the needs of UPAs can be stimulating and inspirational. However, for many of us the nub will come when we realize what the section on finance recommends. The financing of the Report's recommendations to the church grounds all the theory of biblical and social concern for the weak in the hard graft of increased church giving which will enable practical implementation. These proposals affirm both Paul's key passage on giving to the Corinthian Church (2 Corinthians 8.13-14), and the Partners in Mission Report (7:65). They will also bring home to every parish and diocese the cost of commitment to the weak. Supporting ministry and church life in UPAs will then begin to be spread across the whole church rather than being confined to those who live or minister in UPAs. That, in itself, would be a real step forward in the spiritual maturity of the National Church.

(a) Potential Giving

The Report identifies 'giving' as an area in church life that could improve, Giving is 'more a reflection of perceived needs than of church members' overall potential to give' (7:61). We give just enough to cover our budget. rather than giving a positive percentage of what we receive as a thank offering to God. Indeed, where the need is greater in many UPA parishes, the giving is usually higher per person than in other more wealthy areas (7:64). In some dioceses it is high historical resources that appear to be a disincentive to increasing giving amongst present congregations (7:72). Many dioceses and parishes could increase giving which would lead to greater self-sufficiency and less dependence on historic resouces (7:71, 72).

24